GRAPHIC

Ho...

Carol Holliday & Jo Browning Wroe

Illustrated by Bubs Renker

First published in 2016 by
Speechmark Publishing Ltd
2nd Floor, 5 Thomas More Square, London E1W 1YW, UK
Tel: +44 (0)845 034 4610 Fax: +44 (0)845 034 4649
www.speechmark.net

Designed and typeset by Moo Creative (Luton)

002-6012/Printed in the United Kingdom by CMP (uk) Ltd

British Library Cataloguing in Publication Data

A catalogue record for this book is available from the British Library

ISBN 978 1 90930 164 1

Woodland
CARBON
www.woodlandcarbon.co.uk
18CMPUKL
Printed on Carbon Captured paper

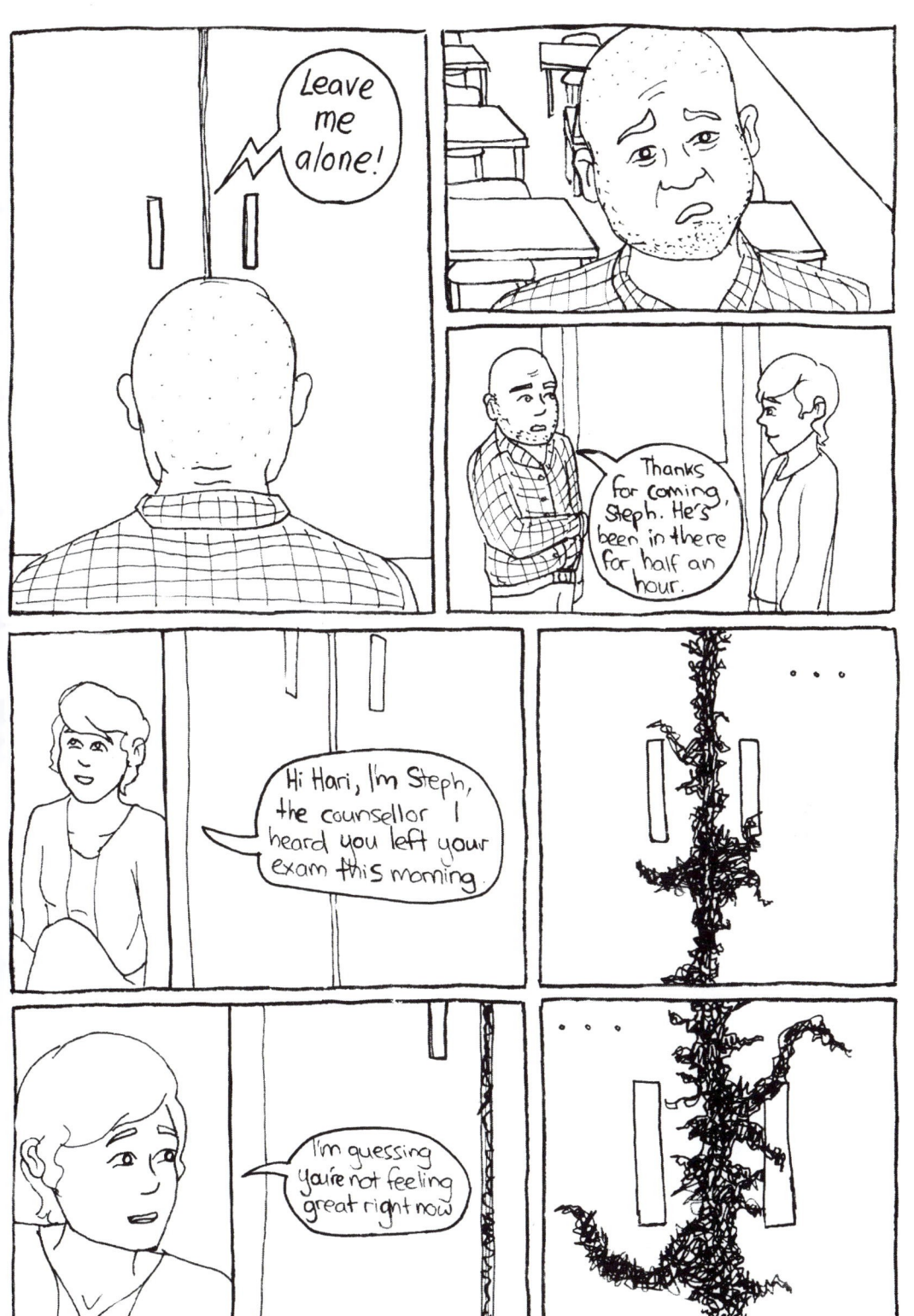

3

5

21

50